Guess Who
Purrs

Dana Meachen Rau

Marshall Cavendish Benchmark
New York

I have soft fur.

I lick it clean.

I have four paws.

My paws have *claws*.

I have *whiskers*.

They help me to feel.

I have two ears.

They turn to hear.

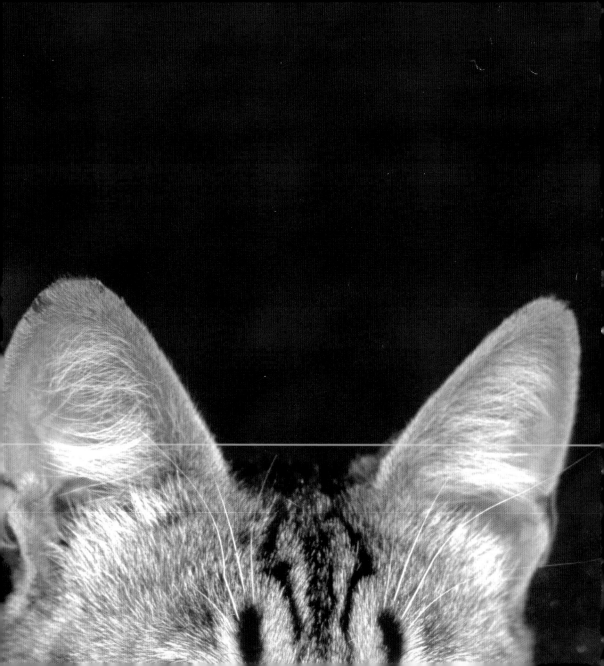

I have two eyes.

I can see at night.

I have a tail.

My tail helps me balance.

I can climb.

I sit up high.

My babies are kittens.

They drink milk from me.

I meow when I am hungry.

I purr when I am happy.

I like to play.

I run and *pounce*.

I sleep a lot.

I *stretch* and yawn.

I rub your leg to say hello.

Who am I?

I am a cat!

Who am I?

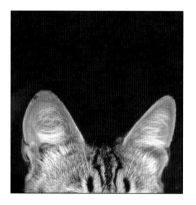

ears

eyes

fur

kittens

paws

tail **whiskers**

Challenge Words

claws (klaws) The sharp, curved nails on a cat's paws.

pounce (pouns) To jump suddenly.

stretch (strech) To reach up or out.

whiskers (WIS-kuhrs) The long, stiff hairs near a cat's mouth.

Index

Page numbers in **boldface** are illustrations.

babies, 16, **17**
balancing, 12

claws, 4, **5**, 29
climbing, 14, **15**

ears, 8, **9**, **28**
eyes, 10, **11**, **28**

feeling, 6
fur, 2, **3**, **28**

hearing, 8

kittens, 16, **17**, **28**

meow, 18
milk, 16

paws, 4, **5**, **28**, 29
play, 20, **21**
pounce, 20, **21**, 29
purr, 18

rubbing, 24, **25**

seeing, 10
sitting, 14
stretch, 22, 29

tail, 12, **13**, **29**

whiskers, 6, **7**, 29, **29**

yawn, 22, **23**

About the Author

Dana Meachen Rau is the author of many other titles in the Bookworms series, as well as other nonfiction and early reader books. She lives in Burlington, Connecticut, with her husband and two children.

With thanks to the Reading Consultants:

Nanci Vargus, Ed.D., is an Assistant Professor of Elementary Education at the University of Indianapolis.

Beth Walker Gambro is an Adjunct Professor at the University of St. Francis in Joliet, Illinois.

Marshall Cavendish Benchmark
99 White Plains Road
Tarrytown, New York 10591-5502
www.marshallcavendish.us

Library of Congress Cataloging-in-Publication Data

Rau, Dana Meachen, 1971–
Guess who purrs / by Dana Meachen Rau.
p. cm. — (Bookworms. Guess who)
Summary: "Following a guessing game format, this book provides young readers with
clues about a cat's physical characteristics, behaviors, and habitats, challenging readers
to identify it"—Provided by publisher.
Includes index.
ISBN 978-0-7614-2972-2
1. Cats—Juvenile literature. I. Title. II. Series.
SF445.7.R36 2009
636.8—dc22
2007024606

Editor: Christina Gardeski
Publisher: Michelle Bisson
Designer: Virginia Pope
Art Director: Anahid Hamparian

Photo Research by Anne Burns Images

Cover Photo by *SuperStock*/Ingram Publishing

The photographs in this book are used with permission and through the courtesy of:
Peter Arnold: pp. 1, 23 BIOS/Herent Sebastien; pp. 5, 28BR PHONE/Thiriet Claudius;
pp. 15, 25 BIOS/Klein & Hubert; p. 27 PHONE/ J.M. Labat. *Animals Animals*: pp. 3, 28TR
Ulrike Schanz; pp. 13, 29L Werner Layer; pp. 17, 28BL Henry Ausloos; p. 21 Robert Maier.
Corbis: pp. 7, 29R Mark A. Johnson. *SuperStock*: pp. 9, 28TL age fotostock;
pp. 11, 28TC Ingram Publishing; p. 19 Photodisc.

Printed in Malaysia
1 3 5 6 4 2